1170 R

Junior Library of Money

SPENDING MONEY

BY RAE SIMONS

RAP 866 4114

MASON CREST PUBLISHERS INC.
370 Reed Road
Broomall, Pennsylvania 19008
(866)MCP-BOOK (toll free)
www.masoncrest.com

First Printing
9 8 7 6 5 4 3 2 1

Library of Congress Cataloging-in-Publication Data

Simons, Rae, 1957–
 Spending money / by Rae Simons. — 1st ed.
    p. cm.
 Includes bibliographical references and index.
  ISBN 978-1-4222-1770-2 (hbk.)   ISBN 978-1-4222-1759-7 (series)
  ISBN 978-1-4222-1889-1 (pbk.)   ISBN 978-1-4222-1878-5 (pbk. series)
1. Consumption (Economics)—Juvenile literature. 2. Money—Juvenile literature. 3. Finance, Personal—Juvenile literature. I. Title.
 HC79.C6.S566 2011
 332.024—dc22
                            2010028155

Design by Wendy Arakawa.
Produced by Harding House Publishing Service, Inc.
www.hardinghousepages.com
Cover design by Torque Advertising and Design.
Printed by Bang Printing.

Contents

INTRODUCTION

Our lives interact with the global financial system on an almost daily basis: we take money out of an ATM machine, we use a credit card to go shopping at the mall, we write a check to pay the rent, we apply for a loan to buy a new car, we set something aside in a savings account, we hear on the evening news whether the stock market went up or down. These interactions are not just frequent, they are consequential. Deciding whether to attend college, buying a house, or saving enough for retirement, are decisions with large financial implications for almost every household. Even small decisions like using a debit or a credit card become large when made repeatedly over time.

And yet, many people do not understand how to make good financial decisions. They do not understand how inflation works or why it matters. They do not understand the long-run costs of using consumer credit. They do not understand how to assess whether attending college makes sense, or whether or how much money they should borrow to do so. They do not understand the many different ways there are to save and invest their money and which investments make the most sense for them.

And because they do not understand, they make mistakes. They run up balances they cannot afford to repay on their credit card. They drop out of high school and end up unemployed or trying to make ends meet on a minimum wage job, or they borrow so much to pay for college that they are drowning in debt when they graduate. They don't save enough. They pay high interests rates and fees when lower cost options are available. They don't buy insurance to protect themselves from financial risks. They find themselves declaring bankruptcy, with their homes in foreclosure.

We can do better. We must do better. In an increasingly sophisticated financial world, everyone needs a basic knowledge of our financial system. The books in this series provide just such a foundation. The series has individual books devoted specifically to the financial decisions most relevant to children: work, school, and spending money. Other books in the series introduce students to the key institutions of our financial system: money, banks, the stock market, the Federal Reserve, the FDIC. Collectively they teach basic financial concepts: inflation, interest rates, compounding, risk vs. reward, credit ratings, stock ownership, capitalism. They explain how basic financial transactions work: how to write a check, how to balance a checking account, what it means to borrow money. And they provide a brief history of our financial system, tracing how we got where we are today.

There are benefits to all of us of having today's children more financially literate. First, if we can help the students of today start making wise financial choices when they are young, they can hopefully avoid the financial mishaps that have been so much in the news of late. Second, as the financial crisis of 2007–2010 has shown, poor individual financial choices can sometimes have implications for the health of the overall financial system, something that affects everyone. Finally, the financial system is an important part of our overall economy. The students of today are the business and political leaders of tomorrow. We need financially literate citizens to choose the leaders who will guide our economy through the inevitable changes that lie ahead.

Brigitte Madrian, Ph.D.
Aetna Professor of Public Policy
and Corporate Management
Harvard Kennedy School

SPENDING MONEY:
What's Really Going On?

Money is such a key part of modern life that it may be easy to take it for granted. But what does money represent? What do all those bills and coins mean? In essence, money represents the time you've spent making it.

Your time, whether spent working in a part-time job or doing chores around the house for an allowance, has value. When you work for money, you're exchanging your time for payment. Whenever you spend money to buy something, you are exchanging money for that item. The value of the item is thought to be equal to what you're paying for it. Think of it this way: you spent time earning money, and then exchange that time you spent working for the products and services you want to buy.

Thinking of money as the time that you spent to make it can help you put spending money into perspective. When you see an item you want to buy, think about how much time it takes for you to make the amount of money that item costs. You might want to buy a DVD, for instance. How many hours of work would it take to make the cost of that DVD? How many chores before you'd have enough to pay for it?

Money and finances can seem overwhelming, especially when you're young and just starting to deal with these ideas. Understanding the value of money is a great way to start to make smart choices when it comes to spending the money you make.

WHAT'S MONEY?

People once bartered—traded—for the items they needed. Even a cow could be considered a valid form of payment.

In North America—before there was any form of money we'd recognize today—clamshells were used as currency because they lasted so long.

Coins, the earliest kind of money used that we'd find familiar today, were first used because they could be easily counted in any amount.

The very first paper money was essentially a promise to pay for something later. Our modern bills carry on the legacy of people using paper money.

BE A WI$E $PENDER

Spending wisely can be difficult. It's easy to see something you want and think that you need to buy it immediately, but consider taking a few seconds to ask yourself some questions.

1. Do I really need this item?
2. If I don't need it, why do I really want it?
3. Will I use it after I buy it?
4. If I buy it now, will I have enough money for things I might need in the near future— this week, this month, next month?
5. If I buy it, will that decision take money away from paying off any debts I owe?
6. Can I put off making a decision about buying it?
7. What are the chances it might go on sale soon?
8. Is it available somewhere else for less money?
9. Could I find an item that is similar, but doesn't carry a brand name? Items without brand names will likely cost less.

Answering these questions for yourself can make the difference between wise spending and impulse buying—often the fastest way to burn through the money you make.

THE ENEMIES OF WISE SPENDING

You might think you're completely to blame if you make a spending decision that you regret, but it isn't always your fault. In fact, many factors are meant to keep you from saving and spending your money in wise ways. Advertising, for one, is designed to get you to spend money. Many ads are meant to separate your sense of wise spending and your desire for the advertised product or service. In addition to advertising, there are many other things that can cause you to spend more, save less, and, ultimately, regret your spending decisions.

The five main enemies of wise spending are:

- Advertising
- Impulse buying
- Shopping for entertainment
- Last-minute shopping
- Mall shopping

Whether you're watching television, surfing the Internet, or reading a magazine, you are seeing advertisements that are trying to get you to spend your money. No matter the product or service that is being advertised, all advertisements are created with the single goal of getting you to part with the money you've earned. This pressure to spend is everywhere, and it can make spending wisely even harder than it already is.

It's important to know that advertising is meant to keep you from thinking logically about making a purchase. The less thought, the better, advertisers think. If you're aware that you are dealing with advertising, you're less likely to buy the advertised product without thinking. Advertising can lead you away from smart spending, but only if you let it.

Impulse Buying

Have you ever been in a store and seen something at the checkout counter that you just had to have? The retail industry places these items carefully so that shoppers see them at the time they are paying for other purchases. These items are usually low in price, making it even easier to simply add a few more things to those you are already buying. Purchasing an item without considering it, based on desire alone, is called impulse buying. The items that are placed around cash registers in almost every kind of store, from supermarkets to clothing stores, are called impulse purchases, or impulse items, and they are meant to tempt you to spend more money than you may want.

Impulse buying can be one of the most challenging parts of shopping and spending money wisely. Resisting your own impulses to buy something can be very difficult and takes a lot of self-control, something the wisest shoppers have developed over time. This sort of self-control doesn't always come easily. You'll have to work at it, but dedicating yourself to spending money thoughtfully is the best way to resist impulse buying.

Shopping and spending your money wisely requires that you think about each purchase you make, each time you spend even a bit of money. If you stop for a second when you find yourself feeling **impulsive** and ask, "Do I really need this?" you are much more likely to make a smart shopping decision. Often, a little thought is all it takes to overcome the pull of impulse buying.

Impulse buying might make you feel good for a short amount of time, but will you regret the purchase later? Will the fact that you spent money on something you didn't necessarily need make you feel worse afterward, when you have less money than you wanted?

Shopping for ENTERTAINMENT

Shopping can be a lot of fun. Hanging out with friends, trying on clothes, looking at the many items stores have available for purchase—all of these things are a part of going shopping, but they can lead you to spend more money than you intend. Often, the more time you spend at a mall or shopping center, the more money you spend. Inside any number of stores, you'll see things you don't need. Sometimes, just seeing something can make you want it, or even make you think you need it. Remember to ask yourself the questions that can help you make smarter buying decisions. Often, thinking through a purchase can help you understand whether you truly need to buy it or not. If you shop as entertainment, you are much more likely to spend money you hadn't planned on spending. You might also make spending decisions that you regret later on.

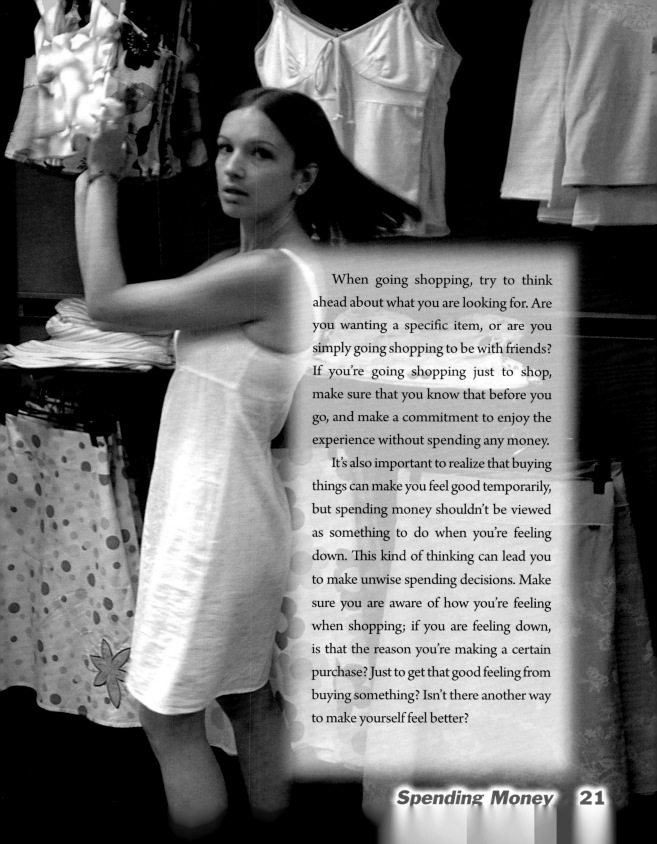

When going shopping, try to think ahead about what you are looking for. Are you wanting a specific item, or are you simply going shopping to be with friends? If you're going shopping just to shop, make sure that you know that before you go, and make a commitment to enjoy the experience without spending any money.

It's also important to realize that buying things can make you feel good temporarily, but spending money shouldn't be viewed as something to do when you're feeling down. This kind of thinking can lead you to make unwise spending decisions. Make sure you are aware of how you're feeling when shopping; if you are feeling down, is that the reason you're making a certain purchase? Just to get that good feeling from buying something? Isn't there another way to make yourself feel better?

Last-Minute Shopping

Imagine that it's the day before your best friend's birthday. You plan on going shopping today, even though you knew her birthday was coming up. Even though you had plenty of time to shop before today, you'll have to go shopping at the last minute if you hope to get her a gift for tomorrow. Shopping in a limited amount of time can prevent you from making the best possible spending choices, and **potentially** could cause you to spend more than you want. Last-minute shopping is rarely the best way to spend your money wisely.

The danger of shopping at the last minute is that you won't be thinking clearly. You might not have planned what to buy, which could lead you to spend more money than you wanted to. Even if you have planned on what to buy, what happens if you try to shop for it when you are under pressure for time and can't find it? You might not have the time to search for the product that you wanted, and instead you might choose to buy a different item, something you hadn't planned on buying.

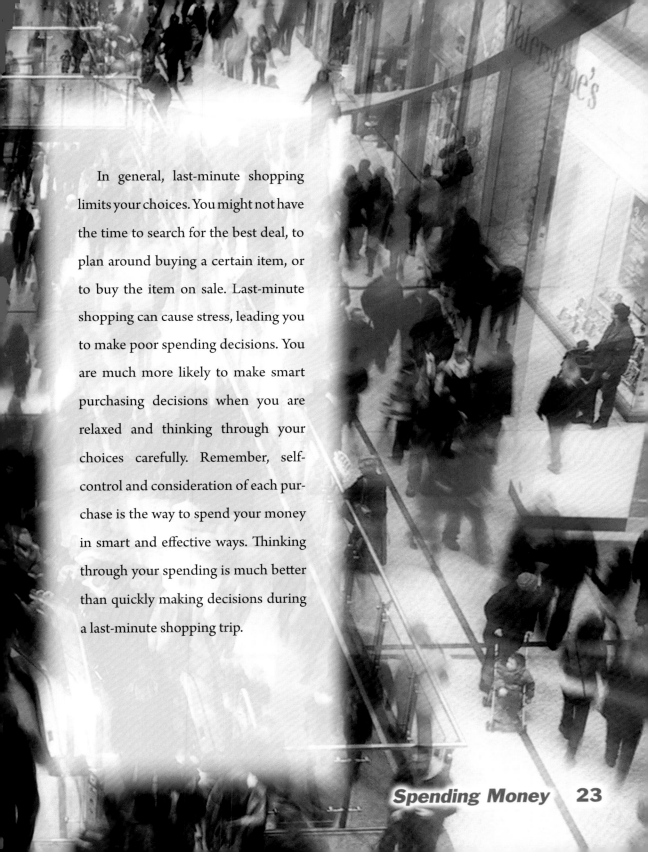

In general, last-minute shopping limits your choices. You might not have the time to search for the best deal, to plan around buying a certain item, or to buy the item on sale. Last-minute shopping can cause stress, leading you to make poor spending decisions. You are much more likely to make smart purchasing decisions when you are relaxed and thinking through your choices carefully. Remember, self-control and consideration of each purchase is the way to spend your money in smart and effective ways. Thinking through your spending is much better than quickly making decisions during a last-minute shopping trip.

MALL SHOPPING

The mall has become a sort of meeting place in modern society, an open area in which people can shop, eat, and spend time together. Hanging out at the mall, however, can lead you to spend more money than you might want, especially as you look at the many products you hadn't planned on buying when you arrived at the mall. Instead of shopping at the mall, try cheaper outlet stores, second-hand clothes shops, and discount retailers. The mall is often much more expensive than these alternatives.

Smart Spending Tips:
SHOP THE SALES

It may seem easy to get caught up in spending money unwisely, but by taking a few steps, by making a few small changes in the way you shop for and buy the items you want, you can make better purchasing decisions and use your money in smarter ways.

As a shopper, you might think that you have very little control over what you pay for the items you want. This is only partly true, however. Though you may never be able to set the price of an item to exactly what you'd like to pay, you can control when you go shopping, which has a lot to do with how much you pay.

The smartest shoppers are also always watching for sales on the items they are looking to purchase. Buying items that are on sale allows you to save some money and also supports a smart spending lifestyle in several ways. First, if you shop for items that are on sale, your shopping will remain focused. To spend wisely, it's always better to know what you want to buy before going shopping. If you've planned to buy an item at a sale, you're more likely to shop with focus. You're less likely to buy things you hadn't planned to when you go shopping for a specific sale item.

On the other hand, it's less beneficial to buy items just because they are on sale. Make sure that the item you're buying on sale is something you really need to buy. Spending more money because you're buying things on sale isn't smart spending.

When it comes to shopping, information is power. When you know how much an item costs at different stores, you're making a more informed decision. In the same way, information about sales is a huge benefit to you, the consumer. If you're shopping and you see an item that you want to buy, try asking a salesperson if it might go on sale in the near future. You might not always get an answer that you like, but you'll know that much more, allowing you to either wait for a sale or make a decision on the spot. An **informed** buyer is a smart buyer. Looking for the best sales isn't the only smart spending tip that can help you spend wisely, though. Using the Internet, keeping a money diary, and making a budget are just a few examples of other smart spending tips.

Smart Spending Tips:
CHEAPER ENTERTAINMENT

Going to the movies can be much more expensive than you might realize. You start by buying tickets, but snacks and drinks can add up, leaving you with less money to spend on other things or put into savings. Finding cheaper entertainment options can be a great way to keep your spending in check.

Instead of going to a theater that charges full price for new movies, for example, why not go to a discount theater? Discount theaters may not play the latest movies as they come out, but they often get these movies later, and always at a cheaper price.

In addition to going to discount theaters, you can save money by going to matinee features, rather than paying the full ticket price. Matinees show before a certain time and are always cheaper than full-priced tickets.

When you go out to the movies or elsewhere, it's easy to spend more money on food and snacks than on the price of the movie or other entertainment . Keeping track of how much money you're spending on these items can be an important way to reduce the amount of money you spend on entertainment. Eating before you go to the movies, for example, might save you a lot of money on food that you might buy at the theater itself.

The local newspaper can be a great resource for finding cheaper entertainment, particularly on the weekends. On Thursdays or Fridays, the newspaper usually contains information on a variety of local weekend activities, many of which are entirely free. In addition, many newspapers may have this information online.

Smart Spending Tips:

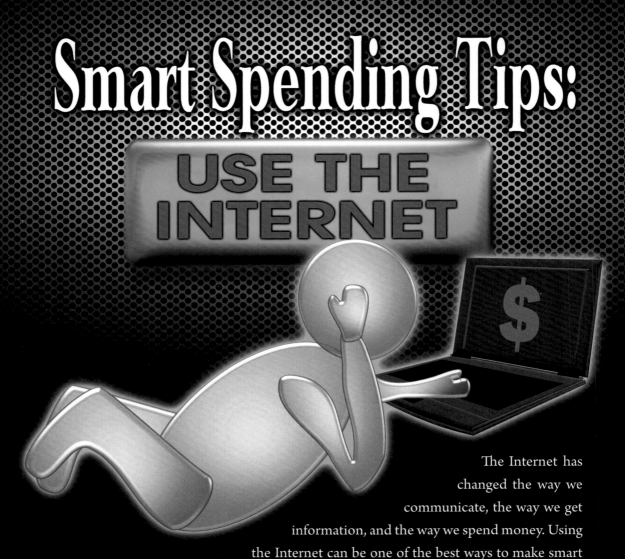

USE THE INTERNET

The Internet has changed the way we communicate, the way we get information, and the way we spend money. Using the Internet can be one of the best ways to make smart buying decisions. On the Internet, you can research the items you want to buy, learning about various models and features. You can also take a look at comments and reviews from other buyers, giving you a good sense of what people who already bought the item think of it. There may also be a number of different retail sites on the Internet that might be selling the product you're looking for, allowing you to compare prices before buying.

Imagine that you want to buy a digital camera. You might search for the camera and find many more results than you'd find stores that carry the same item. The online stores that have the camera will likely give you plenty of information about its features, as well as giving you feedback from users who've got the camera you want. In fact, this information might be more than a store clerk knows about the camera you're shopping for. If one online store has the camera at a certain price, another might have it at a lower price, allowing you to shop around for the best price before you buy. Even if you only use the Internet to do research on the item you want to purchase, that information can really help you when making spending decisions.

Making a Budget

A budget is a kind of plan that outlines how much money you have coming in, how much of it you will spend, and how much money will be left over, for savings or spending on other items in the future. Again, understanding your financial situation is the best way to know just how much money you can spend, how much you actually need to spend, and how much you can save. Use your money diary as a way to see your spending over a certain period of time—a month, for instance—and base your budget around your income and expenses. Make sure to stick to the budget you create so that it helps you save money, making changes when necessary. Looking at your budget, you can also make decisions about where you can save a bit more, as well.

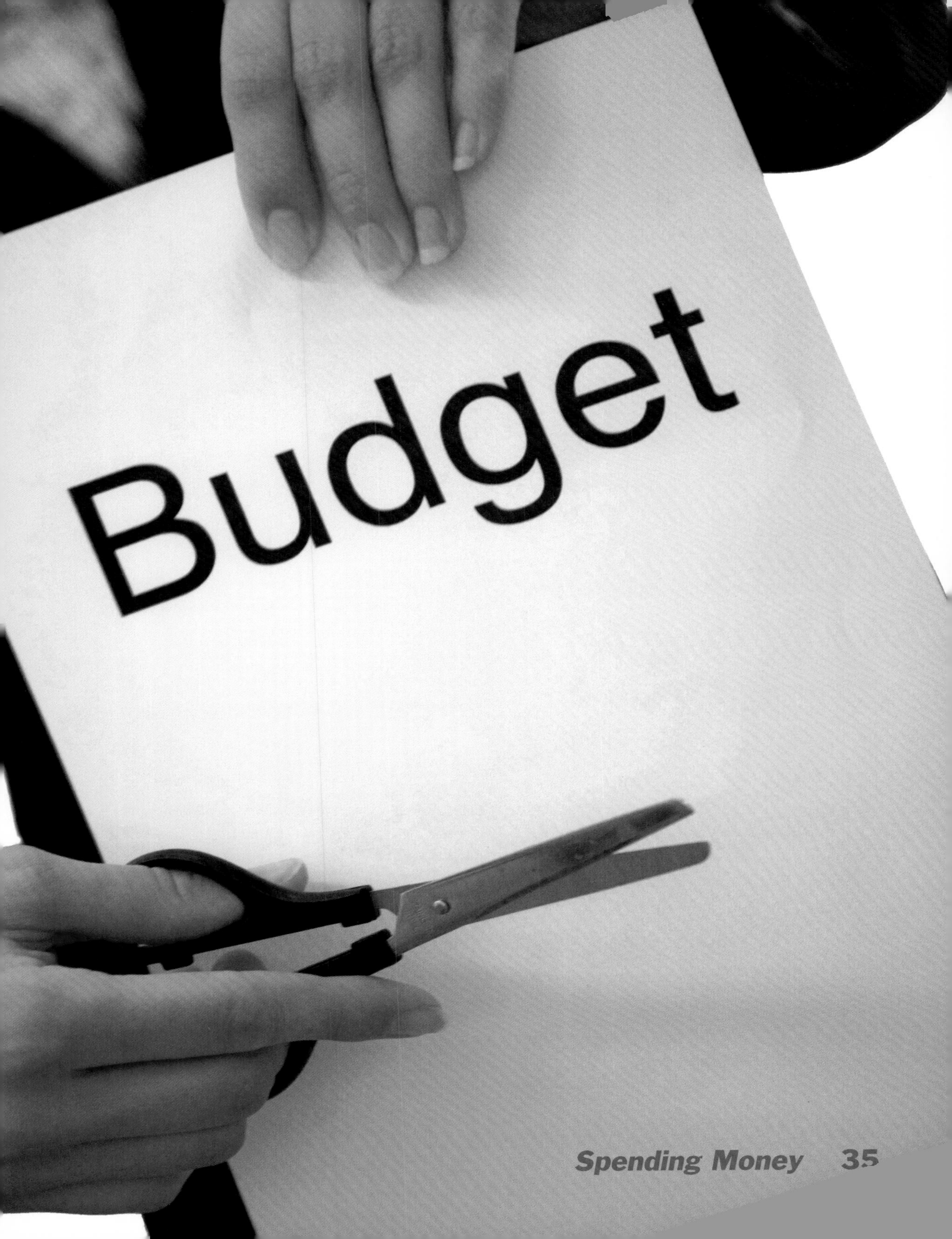
Budget

CASH, CHECK, OR CREDIT?

CASH

Modern money comes in a variety of forms, whether cash, check, or credit. Understanding each of these kinds of money can help you better plan your personal finances and make better spending decisions in general.

Spending cash has many benefits, but it also can present unique challenges. First, when you use cash to pay for your purchases, you aren't running the risk of using money you don't actually have, something that can happen when using credit. Cash is also a physical object, bills and coins in your pocket or hand, rather than a number like the amount of money in your checking account or your credit card balance. It might be easy to spend money from your account when you can't actually see the money changing hands. Out of sight, out of mind, right? With cash, however, you're perfectly aware of how much you're spending and what that amount of money looks like. This can add a sense of value to cash that might be more difficult to understand if you use a card to pay for your purchases.

In addition, some stores will even give discounts to shoppers who use cash to pay for their purchases. This is because these stores have to pay a fee to credit card companies each time someone uses a credit card to pay for their products.

One of the drawbacks of using cash to pay for the items you buy can be the difficulty of keeping track of the amount of money you're spending. It's often easy to have a $20 bill in your pocket at the beginning of the day and then find that money gone by its end. In order to make sure that you know exactly how much you're spending, try to keep all of your receipts. Your receipts can act as **documentation** of your purchases, and you can use the information contained on them to add to your money diary when you get a chance.

Checks

JANE DOE
10 Main Street
Anytown, USA 12345

$\frac{10-4}{222}$ 3622

1922

1
DATE *March 5, 2010*

PAY TO THE ORDER OF *Verizon* **2** $ *66.⁹⁵* **3**

Sixty-six dollars and ⁹⁵/₁₀₀ **4**   DOLLARS 🔒 Security Features Included. Details on Back.

BANK NAME
Anytown

MEMO *phone payment* **6**   *Jane Doe* **5**   MP

⑆ 20 10000 20 ⑆   0 1536798 ⑈ 1922

In order to write a check, you must have a checking account containing at least the amount of money you're writing the check for. When you pay for something using a check, the person or company you're paying will deposit the check in their account, and then that money is taken out of your account. Think of a check as a promise to pay for something. Checks have no value of their own. The money behind that check (in your checking account), however, is valuable. Writing checks is often a good way to make regular payments, particularly for rent or bills. In addition, checks give you a way to easily keep track of the spending you do, something that can help you in your budgeting. A checking account can be a great place to put money, but it won't earn any interest. Interest is a percentage of the money in your account that will be added onto your total balance over time. Try to keep money that you'll need to spend in your checking account and put the rest into a savings account, which will earn interest, allowing you to build your savings.

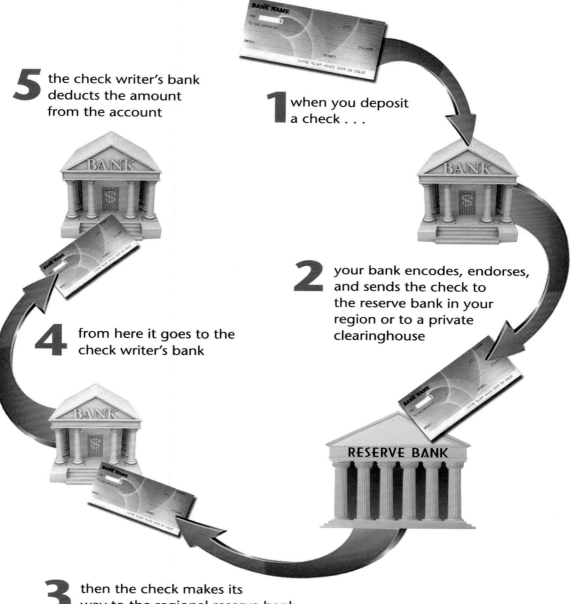

5 the check writer's bank deducts the amount from the account

1 when you deposit a check . . .

2 your bank encodes, endorses, and sends the check to the reserve bank in your region or to a private clearinghouse

4 from here it goes to the check writer's bank

3 then the check makes its way to the regional reserve bank, or clearinghouse for the region where it originated

PLEASE INSERT YOUR
CARD MAGNETIC
STRIPE DOWN. WAIT
FOR THE AUDIO
PROMPT. THEN REMOVE
YOUR CARD.

A debit card looks a bit like a credit card, but it works a little differently. First of all, while credit is money that is not yours that you spend and then pay back, debit cards pull funds directly from your bank account. You can use your debit card to take money out of an ATM and pay for purchases. The amount of money that you take out or spend using your card is then taken from your account.

Keeping Track of Your Checking Account

Number or Code	Date	Transaction Description	Payment Amount		Deposit Amount		$ BALANCE	

In order to write checks and use a debit card, you'll need to open a checking account. As well as opening one, however, you'll need to be responsible for keeping track of your account. When you open a checking account, most banks will give you what is called a check ledger or check register. You can use this ledger to keep track of everything that happens with your checking account. This ledger is also a great way to check for errors in your account. Were you charged too much for a bank fee? Was something accidentally charged to your account twice? These sorts of questions are easy enough to answer by checking your ledger against information that your bank has about your account.

NUMBER OR CODE	DATE	TRANSACTION DESCRIPTION	PAYMENT, FEE, WITHDRAWAL (-)		✓	DEPOSIT, CREDIT (+)		$2382	85
1906	1/4	Bank of America	725	00	✓			725	00
								1657	85
	1/8	DEPOSIT			✓	907	27	907	27
								2565	12
1907	1/11	VERIZON	83	71	✓			83	71
								2481	43
1908	1/12	NYSEG	259	54	✓			259	54
								2221	87
1909	1/12	NY STATE P 76908	200	00	✓			200	00
								2021	87
1910	1/12	BAC MORTGAGE	1189	08	✓			1189	08
								832	79
	1/15	DEPOSIT			✓	1350	00	1350	00
								2182	79
	1/22	DEPOSIT			✓	907	27	907	27
								3090	06
1911	1/28	NYSTATE P76908	200	00	✓			200	00
								2890	06
1912	1/27	DRAINBRAIN	135	00	✓			135	00
								2755	06
1913	1/28	ENDICOTT INTERCONNECT	111	15	✓			111	15
								2643	91

Make sure that you record all activity in your account. The activities that you should be adding to your ledger regularly are:

1. Depositing money in your checking account
2. Writing a check
3. Using your debit card to make purchases
4. Fees charged to your account by the bank
5. Withdrawing money from your account

The challenging part of keeping track of your checking account is making sure to add activities to your ledger as they happen. If you use your debit card or write a check, make sure to put that information into your ledger at that time, rather than waiting until later.

CREDIT

When you use a credit card, you're technically taking out a loan. By using the card, you've agreed that you will pay back whatever amount you're spending. Essentially, credit is borrowed money, all of which you'll have to pay back over time. Not only do you have to pay back the full amount that you used, however, you also must pay interest on the amount you owe. Interest is a percentage of your debt that is added onto what you owe after a debt has gone unpaid for a certain amount of time.

More About Credit and Spending

Credit card companies set the amount of credit you are able to use on your credit card, called your credit limit. If you reach your credit limit, you cannot use your credit card until you pay off the amount you owe. It's important that you pay your monthly credit card bill on time and in full. Often, credit card companies will only ask that you pay a small amount of the money you owe, called the minimum monthly payment. Making only minimum payments can result in additional charges on your account, however, meaning you'll eventually owe more than if you had paid off more than the minimum. Remember that interest is also added to the amount you owe. The interest rate added to your debt is set by the credit card company, based on your ability to pay off debts and use credit wisely.

The Good Things About CREDIT

Credit can be a powerful financial tool that can really help you get the things you want out of life. One of the best things about credit is that if you use it correctly, if you pay off your bill each month and don't let debts pile up, you can build up a solid credit history. Your credit history is something that lenders will look at if you are seeking a loan. Lenders examine how responsible a borrower you are based on how you've used your credit cards, before making a decision as to whether or not they should give you a loan or a low interest rate on a new credit card. A good credit history, meaning that you've paid off your cards on time and haven't run up too much debt, makes you more likely to be approved for a loan in the future. A poor credit history can harm your ability to get loans to pay for the sorts of things you'll need in your life such as a car or home. Building up a good credit history is a great way to get ahead financially.

Credit cards are also helpful in emergencies. If you haven't planned on making a larger purchase, and don't have the cash available at the time, you can use your card to pay for the emergency purchase and pay it off over time. Car repairs, for instance, can be costly, but they are often something that you'll need to pay for quickly so that you can continue to drive. Car trouble is a good example of the kind of emergency spending for which you might use your credit card.

Carrying a credit card is also much safer than carrying loose cash. If you carry cash, you may lose it, or worse, it may be stolen. If your credit card is stolen or lost, however, you can call and tell the credit card company, who will make sure no further purchases go through on your card. You also won't be charged for any purchases that were made after you lost your card or had it stolen. When you lose cash, on the other hand, that money is gone.

The Bad Things About CREDIT

Credit cards can offer financial convenience and security during emergencies. The difficulty of using credit cards is making sure that the amount of credit debt is never more than the amount you are able to pay off each month. Credit cards can be helpful, but they also carry a certain amount of risk.

Unlike cash that you can hold in your hand, credit is less concrete. It might even be hard to make the connection between using a credit card and spending money, since it's not right in front of you when you make a purchase. It's easy enough to let a credit card balance build up without your even knowing it, and suddenly, you're in debt. Worse still, you might not always have the amount of money you need to pay off your credit card debt. You might even mean to pay off your credit card debt in full, but often it's easy to put that payment off. Even though many people carry a balance on their credit card from month to month, it's always best to pay your card off in full each time you are billed.

If you end up letting your debts build, you may begin to damage your credit. By not paying your bills on time, you are not fulfilling your promise to pay back the lenders who've given you the credit card. This information, that you are not being a responsible borrower, is recorded in your payment history, a part of the information that lenders look at to decide whether or not to loan you money. Using credit in irresponsible ways can result in you losing out on the ability to take out a loan when you want to buy a house or car. In addition, a poor credit history means that if you apply for another credit card, you are less likely to get a low interest rate, meaning you'll owe more on the debt on that card. The risk of using credit irresponsibly is that it can prevent you from being able to do the things you want in your life in the future.

KEEP AN EYE ON INFLATION

Imagine that you were able to travel back in time. If you were to take a trip to the 1960s, for example, a movie ticket would only cost you just over one dollar. Today's movies, by contrast, can cost more than ten dollars per ticket, a huge increase over the price of a movie ticket in 1960. In fact, the price of a movie ticket has only ever gone up, decade over decade, year over year. Why? Inflation.

Inflation is the increase in the prices of products and services, which in turn decreases the value of money. Due to inflation, each year the value of a single dollar decreases slightly. A single dollar will buy less ten years from now than it does today because the cost of the items that people purchase will go up.

How does inflation work? Here's an example: If people want to buy more of a certain type of car, the demand for that product increases. The people who want these cars, however, will need to make more money, leading to an increase in salaries for workers. Since the companies that make that type of car will need to pay their workers more to match rising pay, the cost of these cars will go up. This is the inflation cycle. Increased demand leads to higher pay which leads to increased prices and an overall decrease in value of the dollar.

Usually, the rate of inflation is around four percent per year. That means that the price of products and services goes up by four percent every year, forty percent every ten years.

Understanding inflation may seem complicated, but it can also give you an insight into what drives the prices that you pay for the items you purchase. Though the value of your money decreases over time due to inflation, so does the actual value of the money that you owe, your debt. That's right, each year, just as the value of cash decreases, the value of debts decreases in the same way. This decrease in value doesn't necessarily mean you'll pay a lot less on your debts, or that you should keep debts in hopes that inflation works in your favor, simply that inflation has an effect on debt.

Why Be a Wise Spender?

Because Small Savings Add Up

It's important that you always remember that money is a tool that you can use to live the life you want to lead. You are in charge of your finances, they should never be in charge of you. When you decide to make smart spending decisions, you are building a foundation from which you can work toward your ideal financial future.

Spending wisely isn't only about saving money for it's own sake, however. It's also a way to bring security to your life. By spending wisely, you ensure that if an emergency occurs, or you want to make a big change in your life, you're financially able to make the choices you want to, and live your life without worrying about your finances.

Here's What You Need to Remember

- When you work for a paycheck or do chores around the house to get an allowance from your parents, you're exchanging the value of your time for money. Thinking of money as the time you spent working to earn it can help you understand the value of your time, your money, and the things you buy with it. When you spend money on something, think of the time it took to make that amount.

- Often, all it takes to make a smart spending decision is to stop and think about the item you're buying. Do you really need the item? How often will you use it? Can you wait until it goes on sale? Asking yourself a few key questions before buying something can help you avoid a spending decision you'll regret later.

- Advertising, buying things on impulse, shopping for entertainment, shopping at the last-minute, and shopping at the mall can all lead you to make unwise spending decisions. Considering each purchase you make carefully is the best way to make better buying decisions without the negative influence of these enemies of wise spending.

- Whether you're using cash, credit, or checks to pay for the items you buy, each form of money has its own benefits and drawbacks. Knowing about each can help you save and spend in the ways that best suit you.

- Spending your money wisely can be difficult at first, but making smart spending choices when you're young will help put you on a path to financial security in the future.

currency: Any object that has a recognized value and is used as money, in modern times usually coins or bills.

documentation: Something that serves as written proof.

evaluation: The process of determining the value of something.

feedback: Information, reactions, and opinions on something that people share with each other.

impulsive: Something done without planning or considering the consequences.

informed: Having the right information to help you make a decision.

interest rate: The yearly charge for using borrowed money, given as a percentage of the base amount of borrowed money. Interest rates also refer to the amount of money banks annually pay customers to keep their money in savings accounts.

legacy: Something handed down from the past to the present.

potentially: The possibility of happening.

reviews: Opinions, good and bad, about something.

Further Reading

Allman, Barbara. *Banking*. Minneapolis, Minn.: Lerner, 2006.

Blatt, Jessica. *The Teen Girl's Gotta-Have-It Guide to Money: Getting Smart about Making It, Saving It, and Spending It!* New York: Watson-Guptill, 2007.

Byers, Ann. *First Credit Cards and Credit Smarts*. New York: Rosen Publishing, 2009.

Freedman, Jeri. *First Bank Account and First Investments Smarts*. New York: Rosen Publishing, 2009.

Green, Meg. *Everything You Need to Know About Credit Cards and Fiscal Responsibility*. New York: Rosen Publishing, 2000.

Larson, Jennifer S. *Where Do We Keep Money? How Banks Work*. Minneapolis, Minn.: Lerner Classroom, 2010.

Peterson, Judy Monroe. *First Budget Smarts*. New York: Rosen Publishing, 2007.

Wagner, Michael J. *Your Money, Day One: How to Start Right and End Rich*. Charleston, S.C.: BookSurge Publishing, 2009.

Weiss, Anne. *Easy Credit*. Minneapolis, Minn.: Millbrook Press, 2000.

The websites listed on page 61 were active at the time of publication. The publisher is not responsible for websites that have changed their address or discontinued operation since the date of publication. The publisher will review and update the websites upon each reprint.

Find Out More on the

Internet

"Bank Products: What's Insured and What's Not"
www.frbsf.org/publications/consumer/products.html

"Business and Money"
money.howstuffworks.com

"Credit and Charge Cards: What Consumers Should Know About the Cost and Terms of Credits"
www.frbsf.org/publications/consumer/cards.html

"Five Money-Saving Shopping Tips"
www.investopedia.com/articles/pf/07/five-saving-tips.asp

"Fun Facts About Money"
www.frbsf.org/federalreserve/money/funfacts.html

"How to Establish, Use, and Protect Your Credit"
www.frbsf.org/publications/consumer/credit.html

MyMoney.gov
www.mymoney.gov

Young Money Magazine
www.youngmoney.com

Index

Photo Credits

ABOUT THE AUTHOR AND CONSULTANT

Rae Simons is a well-established educational author, who has written on a variety of topics for young adults for the past twenty years. She has also worked with financial advisors to produce adult-level books on money management.

Brigitte Madrian is Professor of Public Policy and Corporate Management in the Aetna-Chair at Harvard University's Kennedy School of Government. She has also been on the faculty at the Wharton School and the University of Chicago. She is also a Research Associate at the National Bureau of Economic Research and coeditor of the *Journal of Human Resources*. She is the first-place recipient of the National Academy of Social Insurance Dissertation Prize and the TIAA-CREF Paul A. Samuelson Award for Scholarly Research on Lifelong Financial Security.